WHAT A BLAST!

WHAT A BLAST!

The Explosive Escapades of Ethan Flask and Professor von Offel

MAD SCIENCE

by Kathy Burkett
Creative development by Gordon Korman

SCHOLASTIC INC.

New York Toronto London Auckland Sydney
Mexico City New Delhi Hong Kong

WHAT A BLAST!
The Explosive Escapades of Ethan Flask and Professor von Offel

ISBN 0-439-22856-5

Published by Scholastic Inc., 555 Broadway, New York, NY 10012.

12 11 10 9 8 7 6   2 3 4 5/0

Printed in the U.S.A.

First Scholastic printing, October 2000

Table of Contents

Prologue

For more than 100 years, the Flasks, the town of Arcana's first family of science, have been methodically, precisely, safely, in other words, *scientifically* inventing all kinds of things.

For more than 100 years, the von Offels, Arcana's first family of sneaks, have been stealing those inventions.

Where the Flasks are brilliant, rational, and reliable, the von Offels are brilliant, reckless, and ruthless. The nearly fabulous Flasks could have earned themselves a major chapter in the history of science — but at every key moment, there has always seemed to be a von Offel on the scene to "borrow" a science notebook, beat a Flask to the punch on a patent, or booby-trap an important experiment. Just take a look at the Flask family tree and then the von Offel clan. Coincidence? Or *evidence*!

Despite being tricked out of fame and fortune by the awful von Offels, the Flasks have doggedly continued their scientific inquiries. The last of the family line, Ethan Flask, is no exception. An outstanding sixth-grade science teacher, he's also conducting studies into animal intelligence and is competing for the Third Millennium Foundation's prestigious Vanguard Teacher Award. With no von Offels around, maybe this time a Flask will get the recognition he deserves. The von Offels risked everything in their maniacal pursuit of science, which is why the family line eventually died out in the 1960s.

Or did it?

Suddenly, there is a new, previously unknown von Offel on the science scene, Professor John von Offel. He bears an uncanny resemblance to the original mad scientist, Johannes von Offel, who blew himself up in 1891 in an attempt to create the world's safest explosive.

The truth is Johannes didn't really die; he just entered an altered state. For decades, von Offel, with reluctant help from his amazing parrot, Atom, has been trying to bring himself fully back to the flesh—and he's 65 percent there. A few more experiments and he'll be whole: no more fading in and out, losing his shadow, or leaving no footprints. To achieve his goal—a real human body—von Offel needs to tap into the sour⟨ scientific ideas that his family has al\ depended upon: he needs a Flask.

That's why Johannes von Offel has transformed himself into his own descendant: Professor John von Offel, the evaluator for the Third Millennium Foundation. The person who'll be interrupting, er, *overseeing* all Ethan Flask's work!

 You'll find step-by-step instructions for the experiments mentioned on pages 42, 43, 44, 56, and 64 of this book in *Explosive Reactions*, the Mad Science experiments log.

The Nearly Fabulous Flasks

Jedidiah Flask
2nd person to create rubber band

Augustus Flask
Developed telephone; got a busy signal

Oliver Flask
Missed appointment to patent new glue because he was mysteriously epoxied to his chair

Marlow Flask
Runner-up to Adolphus von Offel for Sir Isaac Newton Science Prize

Percy Flask
Lost notes on cure for common cold in pick-pocketing incident

Mildred Flask Tachyon
Tranquilizer formula never registered; carriage horses fell asleep en route to patent office

Amaryllis Flask Lepton
Discovered new kind of amoeba; never published findings due to dysentery

Archibald Flask
Knocked out cold en route to patent superior baseball bat

Lane Tachyon
Developed laughing gas; was kept in hysterics while a burglar stole the formula

Norton Flask
Clubbed with an overcooked meat loaf and robbed of prototype microwave oven

Salome Flask Rhombus
Discovered cloud-salting with dry ice; never made it to patent office due to freak downpour

Roland Flask
His new high-speed engine was believed to have powered the getaway car that stole his prototype

Constance Rhombus Ampère
Lost Marie Curie award to Beatrice O'Door; voted Miss Congeniality

Margaret Flask Geiger
Name was mysteriously deleted from registration papers for her undetectable correction fluid

Michael Flask
Arrived with gas grill schematic only to find tailgate party outside patent office

Solomon Ampère
Bionic horse placed in Kentucky Derby after von Offel entry

Ethan Flask

The Awful von Offels

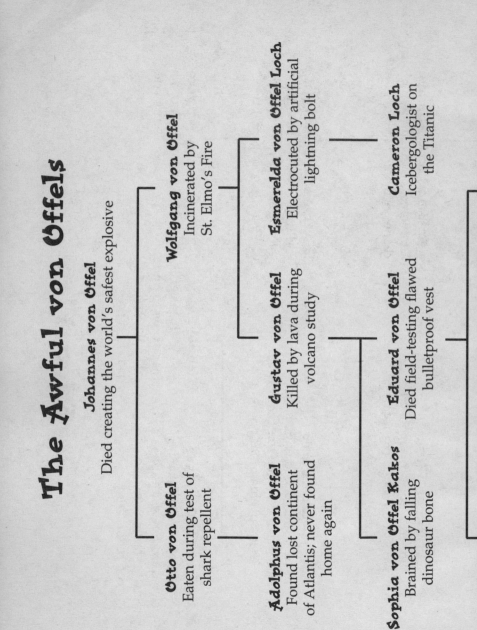

Johannes von Offel
Died creating the world's safest explosive

Wolfgang von Offel
Incinerated by St. Elmo's Fire

Esmerelda von Offel Loch
Electrocuted by artificial lightning bolt

Cameron Loch
Icebergologist on the Titanic

Otto von Offel
Eaten during test of shark repellent

Gustav von Offel
Killed by lava during volcano study

Eduard von Offel
Died field-testing flawed bulletproof vest

Adolphus von Offel
Found lost continent of Atlantis; never found home again

Sophia von Offel Kakos
Brained by falling dinosaur bone

Rula von Offel Malle
Evaporated

Kurt von Offel
Weak batteries in
antigravity backpack

Beatrice Malle O'Door
Drowned pursuing the
Loch Ness Monster

Colin von Offel
Transplanted his brain
into wildebeest

Felicity von Offel Day
Brained by diving bell
during deep-sea
exploration

Feldspar O'Door
Died of freezer burn
during cryogenics
experiment

Alan von Offel
Failed to survive field
test of nonpoisonous
arsenic

Professor John von Offel (?)

Johannes von Offel's
Book of Scientific Observations, 1891

Certain it is that I take many risks in the pursuit of discovery. I have broken every bone in my body at least once, singed off my hair twice, and destroyed my home three times—once blown up, once burned down, and once collapsed. I know as plain as the nine fingers I have left that one day my experiments will cost me my life. But do not mourn for me. Some call it madness; I call it science. And through this mad science, I will live again."

CHAPTER 1

The Awful von Offels?

Johannes von Offel's *Book of Scientific Observations* was the jewel in the crown of the Arcana Public Library. To even take it down from the shelf, Alberta Wong needed a note from her school principal. What's more, two librarians stood guard as she carefully leafed through the journal. Her best friends, Luis Antilla and Prescott Forrester III, looked over her shoulder.

"This is incredible!" Alberta said. "All of these formulas . . . and inventions sketched by Arcana's most brilliant scientist himself."

Prescott leaned closer. "Isn't that a drawing of a guy standing on a roof during a lightning storm? His hat looks like a cooking pot attached to a huge sheet of metal. I'm not a science genius like you guys, but that doesn't seem very safe to me."

"Let's get to the point." Luis said. "What is in that old crackpot's notebook that can help Mr. Flask win the Vanguard Teacher Award?"

"I'm not sure," said Alberta. "But the classroom observer who's coming tomorrow is a Professor

John von Offel. Principal Kepler made a few phone calls and found out that he's somehow related to the von Offels who used to live in Arcana. As Mr. Flask's lab assistants, it's our duty to do everything we can to help him impress Professor von Offel. And right now the only thing we know about the professor is that he's related to Johannes von Offel, who, by the way, was not a crackpot."

"*Not* a crackpot?" Luis cried. "Excuse me, but wasn't he the one who blew himself up while trying to create 'the world's safest explosive'?"

"Yes," Alberta admitted. "But he also invented the 'rubber eight,' the forerunner of today's rubber band." She turned a few brittle pages of the notebook. "Here's his sketch."

"I've seen one of those rubber eights in the Awesome von Offels exhibit at city hall," Prescott said. "It's like Siamese twin rubber bands. The label said you could use it to hold two rolled-up pieces of paper together. Seems silly to me. I mean, did they really need to connect a lot of rolled-up paper back in the 1800s?"

"Well, I heard von Offel stole the idea from Mr. Flask's great-great-great-great-great grandfather, Jedidiah Flask," Luis said. "My father says that Jedidiah invented the rubber band himself."

"But the exhibit had a copy of Johannes's patent," Prescott pointed out.

"The patent goes to whoever gets to the patent office first," said Luis. "I heard that Johannes saw an early version of the rubber band in Jedidiah's laboratory. He ran home, cooked up that ridiculous rubber eight, and rushed to the patent office right away."

"Why didn't Jedidiah go to the patent office earlier?" Prescott asked.

"Jedidiah waited until after he'd finished testing his rubber band for strength and safety—like any responsible scientist," Luis answered. "By that time, the patent office wouldn't let Jedidiah patent the rubber band because it was too similar to Johannes von Offel's stupid rubber eight."

"That's just a rumor," said Alberta. "All anyone knows for sure is that Jedidiah and Johannes started the famous feud between the Flask and von Offel families. For all we know, Jedidiah was just jealous of Johannes's success."

"The von Offels *have* been pretty successful," Prescott agreed. "City hall has tons of their inventions on display. Sophia von Offel Kakos's Sweet Spot Baseball Bat . . ."

"Sophia was a paleontologist!" Luis said. "Where did she learn about baseball bats? From studying the *Pinch-hitta-saurus*? Is it just a coincidence that she lived across the street from Archibald Flask, a physicist who once played in the minor leagues?"

". . . Kurt von Offel's dry-ice machine for converting fog into dew . . ." Prescott continued.

"Now there's a useful invention!" Luis rolled his eyes. "And when Kurt patented it, Salome Flask

Rhombus was experimenting with ways to 'seed' clouds with dry ice and make rain. Is that just a coincidence?"

"He's got a point, Alberta," Prescott said.

"Where's the proof, fellow scientist?" Alberta asked.

"Of course, I don't have any," Luis admitted. "How could I? But Kurt von Offel never did any other work in meteorology. His big goal was to reverse gravity. Remember how he died? He was so eager to test his antigravity backpack that he forgot to check the batteries. When he walked off the roof of the von Offel mansion, he slammed into the backyard with such force that he dug his own grave."

"There was a photo of his headstone at the exhibit," said Prescott. "It read 'He Fought Gravity, and Gravity Won.'"

"All of the von Offels were brilliant," Alberta said. "Even if they were a little eccentric."

"Where did this new Professor von Offel come from, anyway?" Prescott asked. "The city hall exhibit said that the last von Offel died in the 1960s."

Alberta sighed. "No more von Offels. What a great loss to science!"

"The Flasks were the true great scientists of this town, no matter what that city hall exhibit says!" Luis said. "They were the real geniuses, while the von Offels grabbed all the headlines."

4

"Some headlines, too," Prescott said. "I saw one at the exhibit that was three inches high."

"Real scientists do careful, safe science," Luis insisted. "That's why Mr. Flask is such a great teacher. He's fun, but he'd never take any crazy risks."

"Safe, huh?" Prescott pointed out the library's front window. Across the street, the white-coated figure of Ethan Flask teetered atop a forty-foot Plexiglas tower.

CHAPTER 2

In Full Swing

In 33 seconds flat, Luis and Prescott were standing on Ethan Flask's front lawn. It took Alberta 37 seconds because she had to pause and thank the startled librarians.

"Mr. Flask knows exactly what he's doing," Luis said as the three caught their breath. He looked up. "What are you doing, Mr. Flask?" he shouted.

Mr. Flask waved. "Oiling my Foucault pendulum," he answered. With one smooth motion, he reached for a pole mounted next to the tower and slid down to the ground. "Now to get things swinging. Could you give me a hand?" He opened a door and led them inside the tower's clear walls.

In the middle of the tower hung a long steel rod. At the bottom of the rod was a metal weight the size of a cannonball. The group pushed the weight toward one corner. While the lab assistants struggled to hold the weight in place, Mr. Flask tied a string to a small loop on one side. He tied the other end of the string to a loop on the wall.

"Okay, stand back!" Mr. Flask steadied the weight

with his hands. "This requires precision." He lifted a tiny pair of scissors from a hook on the wall. Then he stood with his nose touching the weight.

"Is everyone back?" asked Mr. Flask. "One, two, three . . . launch!" He snipped the string. The weight swung to the opposite corner of the tower. It slowed, changed directions, and began to swing back toward the teacher. The heavy weight barreled toward Mr. Flask's grinning face—then slowed and changed directions a hairbreadth from his nose.

"Wow! That was close," Prescott said.

"Science saves the day!" Mr. Flask said. "I knew the pendulum couldn't hit me. It didn't have enough energy."

Prescott looked at the pendulum, which was swinging powerfully, with no signs of stopping. "Okay, it's moving. I guess that means it has energy. But where's the energy come from? I don't see any electric cords."

"Actually, the four of us gave it energy," Mr. Flask replied.

"You mean when we pulled the weight to one side?" Alberta asked.

Mr. Flask nodded. "That gave it potential energy. When I let it go, it became *kinetic* energy—or energy in motion. That energy powered the pendulum's swing. The more kinetic energy, the higher the swing. We gave the weight only enough energy to make it swing this high." He pointed to his nose. "So my face was safe."

"How long will this pendulum swing?" Luis asked. "Until it runs out of energy?"

"You got it!" Mr. Flask answered. "Moving through the air robs the pendulum of some energy; so does friction."

Alberta asked. "But the weight isn't dragging on the ground or anything. Doesn't friction mean rubbing?"

"The pendulum is attached to the tower using a ball joint," Mr. Flask said. "In fact, your leg is attached to your body much the same way." He cupped one hand and turned his other fist inside it. "When the pendulum moves, the top of it rubs the inside walls of the ball joint. That results in friction, which robs the pendulum of energy. The more friction, the more energy lost."

"Ah, that's why you were oiling the top of the pendulum!" Luis said.

Mr. Flask gave him a thumbs-up. "Less friction means less energy lost," he said. "That means the pendulum swings longer. And *that's* when the really cool stuff begins."

"But the pendulum seems to be doing exactly the same thing it did when we first launched it," Prescott said.

"Observe!" Mr. Flask said. "The pendulum *is* still swinging in the same direction—from this corner to that, and back again. However, if you came back tonight, you'd find it swinging between the other two corners. *But* the interesting thing is that it won't really have changed direction at all."

"How can that be?" Prescott asked. "The only way that could happen is if the ground moved underneath it. That's not likely."

"Oh?" Mr. Flask raised his eyebrows and smiled.

Alberta thought for a moment. "The Earth revolves or turns on its axis," she said. "So the tower, the lawn, the house—they all change direction."

"Since we think of those things as staying still, it seems like the pendulum has changed direction," Luis added. "But it's really the other way around."

"Exactly!" Mr. Flask said.

"The Earth isn't the only thing that's turning," Prescott said. "All this science makes my head spin." He sat down on a big rock. "Whoa!" Prescott flipped head over heels as his "rock" stood up.

"Oops! Watch out for Peggy," Mr. Flask laughed, giving Prescott a hand up. The boy stared at a huge spur-thigh tortoise, which slowly lumbered toward the house. "This tower heats up like a greenhouse, so Peggy likes to hang out inside," Mr. Flask said. "But now she's telling me it's tortoise feeding time. Want to help?"

Prescott hesitated, but Luis pressed him toward the front porch with the others.

"Watch the red rat snakes," Mr. Flask warned, stepping over two richly patterned snakes sunning themselves on the porch. Prescott shuddered. The snakes slithered out of the way to let the tortoise pass. Peggy plodded through the open front door and down the hallway.

"How long have you had Peggy?" Alberta asked as they followed.

"I grew up with her. My Aunt Margaret rescued her when the von Offel mansion was deserted." Mr. Flask gestured toward a run-down, three-story house next door. "One of the von Offels must have picked her up on a trip to Africa. My guess is Beatrice Malle O'Door, who was well known for collecting animals from exotic locations."

"Wasn't she the one who drowned chasing the Loch Ness Monster?" Luis asked.

"Well, yes." Mr. Flask led the way to the kitchen. "Or rather, it's true that she drowned in that famous Scottish lake. But did she get scientific proof of the Loch Ness Monster, as her journals insist? I'm no authority, but I always thought her blurry 'monster' photo looked an awful lot like a sock puppet." He smiled and turned to study the contents of a huge refrigerator. "Ah, here we go." He pulled out a huge bowl of greens and set it in front of the tortoise.

Next, Mr. Flask picked up a plastic bin full of boxes and canisters from the kitchen counter, and led the way to the sunny front room. Two of its walls were covered from floor to ceiling with cages and aquariums. As Mr. Flask entered, the whole room began buzzing, clicking, and bubbling with excitement. An elf owl on a tall perch opened a sleepy eye. A beaver waddled across the room and deposited a stick in front of the door.

"She's always trying to dam up the doorway." Mr. Flask laughed. He crossed to a large tank. Inside, dozens of sea horses clung to swaying strands of sea grass. He tapped some flakes into the tank.

"What do you feed the bees?" Luis asked. He stood in front of a clear plastic box that was buzzing with worker bees.

"They can crawl through a tube to get outside into the garden," Mr. Flask explained, "so they can collect nectar from the flowers. But I also give them a little sugar water." He showed Luis how to pour it in.

"Why doesn't this cage have a water bottle in it like all the others?" Alberta asked.

"Those kangaroo rats are native to the desert." Mr. Flask opened the top of the cage. "They get all the water they need from the foods they eat." He dropped in a slice of cactus and a handful of seeds.

"Hey, aren't these frogs beautiful?" Alberta asked.

Prescott leaned closer to the tank. "They are kind of cute." He tapped on the side, and a bright blue-and-black frog turned toward him. "Come closer, little guy."

Alberta stepped up, too. "Poisonous frogs are always so colorful!" she said.

"Poisonous?" Prescott jumped back and scanned the rest of the room nervously. "Is anything else here poisonous?" he asked.

"Only the coral snake," Mr. Flask replied. He dropped some chunks of meat into a tank of piranhas. "Oh, and those black widows in the corner."

"Thanks for the heads up," Prescott said. He headed for the opposite corner. Alberta was already there, looking out of a window at the old von Offel mansion.

"Mr. Flask, is it true that we'll be meeting a real live von Offel?" Alberta's voice sounded dreamy. Luis rolled his eyes.

"I haven't met Professor John von Offel yet," Mr. Flask replied. He opened the window and put out a bowl of greens and fruit. Two wallabies in the yard hopped over. "But if he really is a long-lost von Offel descendant, we should give the Professor a chance."

"But, Mr. Flask," Luis said, "those von Offels were really awful to your family."

"Of course, I grew up hearing stories about the von Offels and their foul play," Mr. Flask said. "And honestly, I have to believe that at least some of them are true. How else can you explain my ancestors' incredible run of bad luck? I mean, Oliver Flask is stuck to his chair for a week, so Otto von Offel beats him to the superglue patent. Mildred Flask Tachyon's carriage horses fall asleep on the way to the patent office, so Adolphus von Offel beats her to the tranquilizer patent. Norton Flask is clubbed with an overcooked meat loaf, and while he lies unconscious, Kurt von Offel gets the microwave

12

oven patent. Even the most skeptical scientist has to see a pattern in that evidence."

Mr. Flask stared at the von Offel mansion next door. "Still, the professor didn't choose his relatives, so let's give him a chance. Maybe *this* von Offel is just a regular guy," he said half heartedly.

Just then, a huge moving van groaned to a halt in front of the von Offel mansion. Two burly movers climbed out of the cab and swung open the door at the back. The movers pulled out an ancient-looking wooden trunk and started dragging it toward the dilapidated front door.

Prescott cringed. "The professor's not really going to live in that dump, is he?"

CHAPTER 3

Welcoming Committee

"Well, I guess we should go over and welcome the professor to Arcana," Mr. Flask said. He opened a cupboard. "We can bring a jar of honey as a housewarming gift, courtesy of the bees."

When the four stepped outside, one mover was pushing a huge wooden chair through the door of the von Offel mansion. There were bands of metal where the sitter's ankles and wrists would be. The second mover followed with a moth-eaten stuffed shark. Dangling from its mouth was a life preserver that read *Titanic*.

"Family heirlooms, I guess," Prescott gulped.

The second mover was struggling with a huge stack of boxes. He put them down and scratched his head.

"It's the weirdest thing," he said as they approached. "Listen." He picked up a box and took a few steps toward the door.

"Hey, careful, buddy!" said a muffled voice. " I'm no spring chicken, you know!"

"Hear that?" said the mover. "You don't suppose . . . nah."

Mr. Flask and his lab assistants followed the mover up the front steps. Mr. Flask stopped just inside the front door. "Hello? Professor von Offel?" His voice echoed down the dimly lit hall.

Luis poked his head into the first room on the right. "Look at this setup!"

"We probably shouldn't . . ." Mr. Flask began, as the lab assistants pushed past him. But when he looked inside, his jaw dropped.

The room was jam-packed with lab tables. All of them were covered with dusty equipment: Bunsen burners, test tubes, microscopes, and petri dishes. A corner cabinet held hundreds of bottles of chemicals. A ring of high shelves held examples of amateur taxidermy, with some freakish results: a wolverine with the tail of a Komodo dragon; a Tasmanian devil with a swordfish's head; a sloth with eagle wings.

"There weren't any of *those* in the city hall exhibit," Prescott said.

Alberta looked around in wonder. "Think of all of the science that went on within these walls."

"Looks like the science went *into* these walls, too," Luis said. He put his fist inside a huge hole in the plaster. "I wonder if this is from the antigravity cannonball."

Alberta pressed her shoe against a mound of volcanic rock. "This could be where Gustav von Offel spilled red-hot lava on his ingrown toenail!"

15

"Don't these look like claw marks around this window?" Prescott asked. "Let's get out of here."

"This is fascinating stuff," Mr. Flask said. "But let's wait until we meet the professor and ask him for a house tour." He led the way to the front hall.

"Get me out of here!"

"Don't worry, Prescott. We're going." Mr. Flask turned toward Prescott. "You sound funny. You didn't open any of those bottles of chemicals, did you?"

Prescott looked startled. "I didn't say anything. I think it came from up there." He pointed to a rickety staircase.

"Should we investigate?" Luis asked.

"It *was* a cry for help," Alberta said.

They all looked at Mr. Flask. "Professor von Offel?" he shouted.

There was no answer.

"We haven't even been invited in here," Mr. Flask said. He looked down at the jar of honey still in his hand. "But Alberta is right. Someone may be in danger."

Prescott looked at the staircase. It was missing half of the guardrail. "The movers can deal with it—whatever it is. Let's go!"

Luis peeked out the front door. "I don't see their moving truck. They must have finished up."

"We have to act," Alberta said. "Besides, this house is just full of history. It's not like it's haunted or anything."

"Unpack me, blast you!" The voice sounded far off and muffled.

"Okay, I can't ignore that," Mr. Flask said. "You three stay down here."

"No way!" Prescott cried. He looked back at the glassy eyes of the wolverine with the dragon tail. "Let's stick together."

"Fine," Mr. Flask said, "but there's nothing to be scared of here." He led the way up the stairs.

The first room at the top of the stairs had once been a bathroom. Pipes for a toilet still poked out from the wall. Now an enormous, empty fish tank filled the room. Snorkels and fins, their rubber cracked and decaying, hung from pegs on the wall.

In the middle of the second room was a long table. A large light fixture hung overhead. A cart topped with sharp, rusty instruments sat to one side. The linoleum floor, originally white, was stained with big, reddish-brown spots.

"Looks just like my dentist's office," Prescott joked.

"This must be Colin von Offel's laboratory," Alberta said. "He was what I guess you'd call an experimental surgeon."

"I think the word you're looking for is unlicensed," Luis replied. "He lost his medical license after he tried to graft a piece of sheepskin coat onto a Chihuahua."

"It was a bold attempt to cure baldness," Alberta

argued. "Okay, so it failed. But the dog pulled through."

"It developed severe wool allergies," Luis replied. "Then not only was the dog hairless, but it couldn't even wear one of those little doggie sweaters. Its owners had to move to Miami."

"Shhh!" Mr. Flask whispered. "After all, the professor could show up at any moment, and that's his ancestor you're talking about. No sign of trouble here. Let's check the next room."

The third room was crammed with boxes and trunks. Some were covered with years' worth of dust. But one pile looked like it had just arrived.

"Anybody home?" Mr. Flask called out. He looked around. "None of these new boxes is big enough for a person to be stuck in. And how could someone have opened one of those trunks without leaving handprints in the dust?"

Luis circled the pile of new boxes. "Oh! I think I found our someone—only it's a *something*." He pointed to an old-fashioned machine with a crank on the side and a huge horn on top.

"What's that?" Prescott asked.

"A phonograph," Mr. Flask answered. "It's kind of an ancient CD player. You wind it up and that disc turns around. A needle picks up sounds from the disc and that big horn amplifies the sounds."

"Maybe it hadn't wound down completely," Luis said. "Maybe something bumped it, and the disc turned for a moment."

"But we clearly heard a cry for help," Prescott said. "Not some old music."

Mr. Flask smiled. "The human brain can be lazy. Sometimes it makes us hear what we want to hear."

"Huh?" Prescott said.

Mr. Flask smiled. "Does this sound familiar: 'But, Mr. Flask, you said that wouldn't be on the test'?"

The lab assistants laughed.

"So, say you're a little nervous about being in the house uninvited," Mr. Flask continued. "The boxes shift, the phonograph needle slips, and ta-da! We think we hear a cry for help."

"Mystery solved!" Alberta said.

Prescott looked unconvinced. "Okay, whatever, let's just get out of here."

Just then, a side door flung open. A strange figure burst in wielding a shovel like an ax.

"Interlopers!" the man shrieked.

"Wait, you've misunderstood," Mr. Flask said, herding the kids back toward the hallway. "We're here to welcome . . ."

"Abandon a house for a few decades and everybody thinks they can wander in!"

"We heard a voice," Alberta tried to explain.

The man jabbed toward them with the shovel.

"We brought honey . . ." Mr. Flask said, holding out the jar.

"Get out!" the man screamed, running at them.

CHAPTER 4

Birdbrains

"Wow! That was a close call yesterday. If that wacko professor hadn't tripped on that pile of molecular models, we'd have all been shoveled to death," Prescott said. He, Alberta, and Luis settled into their seats for science class. "At least then I wouldn't have to find out my grade on our last quiz," he added.

"I don't see any papers on Mr. Flask's desk," Alberta said. "Maybe he didn't grade them. Maybe he was still a little shaken up from our visit with Professor von Offel."

"Our *visit*?" Prescott cried. "You make it sound like we stayed for tea. I did get covered with honey when that jar shattered, but I don't think that counts."

"Doesn't our experience prove that this von Offel is completely crazy, just like all his ancestors?" Luis asked Alberta.

"Genius is often misunderstood," Alberta replied stubbornly.

"What part of 'If I catch you here again I'll kill

20

you!' did we not understand?" Prescott asked. "I thought the professor came in loud and clear."

The bell rang, and there was a noisy beating of wings outside of the open windows. A carrier pigeon fluttered in and landed on Mr. Flask's desk. Then came another, and another, until three-dozen carrier pigeons covered his desk, the chalkboard tray, and a table with the class's human organ models.

"Mr. Fla-ask! There's a pigeon on my gallbladder!" came a whiny voice from behind Prescott.

Mr. Flask reached toward the offending pigeon, and it stepped onto his palm.

"Your model gallbladder is safe, Max, I promise," Mr. Flask said.

Max Hoof was not satisfied. "Papier-maché is very delicate," he grumbled.

Mr. Flask slid a piece of paper out of a tube attached to the bird's leg. He unrolled it.

"And here's your graded quiz, Max." Mr. Flask handed it over. "Nice job, too."

Alberta raised her hand.

"Did that bird know it had Max's paper? Is that why it landed on Max's model?" she asked.

Mr. Flask removed a quiz from a second bird's tube. "I think it was just a coincidence, but that's a good question. Scientists are always learning new and surprising things about animal intelligence. It turns out that birdbrains have an unfair reputation. Some birds are pretty smart." He looked down at the paper. "Prescott, here's yours."

Prescott held his breath and unrolled his quiz: 87, a solid B. "Whew!" he sighed.

Mr. Flask held up another paper. "Sean, how did your quiz get so sticky? Just because the topic was sugars and carbohydrates doesn't mean I needed specimens."

Sean Baxter grabbed his quiz. "Hey look, I got the same grade as you." He poked Prescott with his paper. "Guess I could be a lab assistant, too."

"Grow up, Sean," muttered the cool voice of Heather Patterson. For once Sean stayed quiet. Prescott blushed deeply, which made Alberta roll her eyes. Why was it that every boy melted around Heather Patterson?

The door swung open, and the principal entered. Everyone stared at Dr. Kepler, and the strange, rumpled figure behind her. Alberta smiled brightly, Luis rolled his eyes, and Prescott slunk down in his chair. Mr. Flask stepped back and motioned for Dr. Kepler to take center stage.

"Students, I know that you share my pride in having our star science teacher, Mr. Flask, named as a finalist for the Third Millennium Foundation's prestigious Vanguard Teacher Award," Dr. Kepler began. "Science is an important subject at Einstein Elementary School, and we're honored to have such an enthusiastic and innovative teacher. We're also honored to welcome a long-lost son of Arcana, Professor John von Offel. He'll be visiting your classroom to evaluate Mr. Flask's teaching methods for the foundation." She turned toward the rumpled figure and smiled warmly. "Professor von Offel meet Mr. Flask. Mr. Flask, Professor von Offel."

Mr. Flask stepped forward to shake the professor's hand. "I believe we've . . ."

Professor von Offel cut him off. "Oh, it's you." He scanned the class, and his eyes fell on Prescott, then Luis, then Alberta. "I see," he said.

There was an awkward silence broken by a flapping sound. Mr. Flask looked toward the classroom door and said, "Professor, my class and I have an ongoing study of animal intelligence." He pointed to the cages and tanks around the room. "We'd really be very interested in meeting your parrot."

On cue, a battered green bird fluttered in from the hallway and landed on the professor's shoulder. He preened himself proudly.

"There's nothing unusual about this bird's intelligence," the professor said. The parrot reached over and nipped his neck. The professor twitched.

"Aren't parrots one of the most intelligent species of birds?" Dr. Kepler asked. She looked puzzled.

"Oh, er, yes." The professor took on a formal tone. "Students, this is Atom. Not only are parrots relatively intelligent—for birds—but some of them are also extremely long-lived. This specimen is a hundred-thirteen years old." He held the bird up grandly.

There was an excited cooing and fluttering. Then all three-dozen pigeons flew at the parrot with their claws extended.

Atom darted out of the professor's hand and took off toward the cages along the back wall. The agitated pigeons followed.

"Stay away from me!" the parrot squawked.

As he landed on each cage, the animals inside went wild. The snakes reared up and hissed. The mice bit the sides of their cages with sharp white teeth. The bullfrogs chorused noisily. Meanwhile, the pigeons kept flying at Atom from every side.

Atom finally dived toward a human skeleton in the corner. He scrambled up inside the rib cage. Mr. Flask shooed the pigeons out of the window.

"I don't know what got into them," Mr. Flask apologized to the professor and Dr. Kepler. He held his finger out for Atom to perch on. "Are you okay, little guy?"

Atom fluttered past Mr. Flask's finger and onto the ground. He walked across the classroom with his beak in the air. Then he flew up and perched on the professor's shoulder.

"You know," Dr. Kepler said, "it almost sounded as though he was yelling at the pigeons."

All eyes turned toward Atom. He gulped. "Awk! Stay away! Stay away! Awk! Awk!"

"Nothing but ordinary parrot talk," the professor said. He narrowed his eyes at Atom.

Prescott leaned toward Alberta and Luis. "That bird is as weird as the professor!" he whispered.

"Haven't we heard that parrot's voice somewhere before?" Luis asked.

Alberta's mind was elsewhere. "Do you have any idea how good it will look on a college application if we were taught by a real von Offel?" she whispered.

"College? We're only in sixth grade!" Prescott said. Alberta ignored him and raised her hand. "Dr. Kepler, could the professor teach us a science lesson—as a kind of introduction?"

"That's a wonderful idea!" Dr. Kepler turned to the professor. "Will you do us the honor?"

The professor nodded and fished an old-fashioned monocle out of his pocket. He studied its reddish-iron frame with disapproval. "Rust!" he muttered. Then he strode to the front of the classroom.

Alberta smiled at him encouragingly.

"I will lecture today on the single most destructive category of chemical reaction." The professor held out his rusty-framed monocle. "I speak, of course, of the breed of oxidation-reduction reactions more commonly known as corrosion. Of corrosive reactions, one of the most frequently observed in our industrial age is the process by which the metal, iron, transforms, in the presence of water vapor, into ferric oxide, or rust."

The professor paused to write on the board. Prescott looked confused; Luis looked bored; Sean was already sleeping, his jaw slack. Alberta blinked to keep her eyes open. Luis caught her eye and mouthed the word "awful."

"Maybe he just needs a little time to warm up,"

she whispered to Luis. But she didn't sound very sure.

The professor scribbled on the board with his chalk. He wrote:

$$Fe^{+2} + 2OH^{-1} \longrightarrow Fe(OH)_2$$
$$4Fe(OH)_2 + O_2 \longrightarrow 2(Fe_2O_3 + 2H_2O)$$

"Most oxidation-reduction reactions are, by nature, exothermic," the professor droned. "This is the case whether they be corrosive or combustive. The rate at which the heat is dispersed depends on the specific reaction."

Sean snored softly. On the other side of the classroom, someone's head hit the desk. Even Alberta was holding her chin in her hands to stay awake.

Sean shifted in his sleep and snorted loudly. The professor was startled, and his chalk hit the floor.

"Did you see that?" Prescott whispered to Alberta.

"Huh? What?"

"The chalk! It went right *through* the professor's hand!"

Alberta stifled a yawn. "You're seeing things. The professor just dropped it."

Prescott shook his head. "I know what I saw!" he said.

Dr. Kepler, still standing by the door, cleared her throat loudly.

Mr. Flask stepped forward with a big smile.

"Great suggestion, Professor! Class, tomorrow we'll begin experimenting with explosions."

Explosions? Sean was jarred out of his slumber. Students all over sat up straighter.

"But I thought the professor was talking about rust," whined Max.

"Shh!" hissed all the students around him.

Mr. Flask nodded. "Well, Max, as the professor said, rust and chemical explosions have a lot in common."

A murmur went through the class. "Is *that* what he said?"

"Rust—fire—exploding fireworks—all are *exothermic* chemical reactions. That simply means that they give off heat," Mr. Flask explained. "It's no surprise that fire gives off heat, right? But rust does, too. It just happens so slowly that you can't feel it."

"What about explosions?" Sean shouted out. He was wide awake now.

Mr. Flask continued. "A lit firework releases heat incredibly quickly. All of that heat causes the air to expand superfast. What happens when air expands quickly? Let's do a little experiment."

Mr. Flask reached into the top drawer of his desk and pulled out a balloon. "Luis, could you inflate this?"

Luis took a big breath and blew. The balloon puffed up a bit, but it didn't get any bigger.

"Hey, Luis," Sean called. "Need a smaller balloon?"

"That's an interesting scientific question, " Mr. Flask said. "Is it easier to blow up a bigger balloon or a smaller one? Someday we'll do that experiment. I think you might be surprised, Sean."

Alberta raised her hand. "I blew up about a hundred balloons for my cousin's birthday party. My aunt showed me how to stretch them first. That makes them easier to blow up."

Luis nodded and stretched the balloon like taffy. Then he took another deep breath.

Mr. Flask smiled. "Let's observe Luis's face as he blows up that balloon. His cheeks are puffed out. He's working hard. That's because he's pushing a lot of air into a little space." He took the balloon from Luis and tied it off. "The air inside this balloon is tightly packed, or *compressed*." He took a pushpin from the bulletin board. "When I break the balloon skin with this pin, the air inside will suddenly expand. Any predictions?" He held the pinpoint near the balloon.

All the sixth graders raised both hands—to cover their ears. Mr. Flask laughed. "The prediction is unanimous. Let's test it."

The balloon burst with a resounding boom just as the bell rang.

"We'll do some more explosive experiments tomorrow." Mr. Flask turned toward the professor. "Let's give our guest lecturer a round of applause."

There was a little feeble clapping as the students gathered their books. As they filed out, Mr. Klumpp, the school custodian, fought his way into the classroom. He eyed the room suspiciously. He was clearly checking to see how much mess the sixth grade science class had made today. Mr. Flask gave him a friendly smile and began picking up the pieces of broken balloon skin himself. Mr. Klumpp crossed his arms and glared at the science teacher.

As the professor watched the last students leave, he sniffed his disapproval. "Is that how you teach science, Flask? By making your lesson up as you go along?"

Dr. Kepler tried to smooth things over. "Professor, your introduction to explosions certainly opened up a whole new realm of study. And you'll see that Mr. Flask's experiments always make science real for his students."

Mr. Klumpp muttered, "Yeah, a real pain and a real mess."

CHAPTER 5

The "World's Only Genius Parrot"

Atom paced the length of the small office Dr. Kepler had given the professor. "Flying rats!" he squawked. "That's what pigeons are."

"You almost got us into trouble in there with your talking. Better watch your beak," the professor said.

"It's not my fault I can talk," Atom said. "I'd be living a normal, happy-go-lucky parrot life if not for one of your failed experiments."

"That was a hundred years ago!" the professor replied. "Besides, that extra brain power was meant for me. Those electrical wires were still in my ears seconds before the lightning bolt hit. But you had to go and yank the wires out."

"They looked like spaghetti," Atom said. "I was hungry."

"Well, you slurped up the full impact of the electrical charge," said the professor. "That lightning surge was to have lit up the inside of my skull, awaking parts of my brain that had never before been active."

"I can tell you, it felt more like being buzzed by a chain saw than being lit up like a lightbulb," said Atom.

"Well, I wouldn't know. I was never lucky enough to catch a second lightning bolt," the professor said.

"Well, that electrical charge sure jump-started my career," said Atom. "I became 'The World's Only Genius Parrot.'"

"Some job," the professor said. "Riding from town to town in a run-down circus trailer. Dressed up in a whole flock of absurd costumes. Those tight pants . . ."

"Chicky Martin! One of my hottest impersonations," Atom objected.

"That ridiculous black wig and tiny white jumpsuit . . ."

"Eggvis Presley! I had 'em weeping in the aisles with 'Love Me Tender'!"

"The little white lab coat . . ."

"The famous scientist Albird Einstein!"

"Who's he?" the professor asked.

"He was after your time," said Atom.

"Well, you should thank me for taking you out of that sideshow and giving you a nice, comfortable home," the professor said.

"You owed me," said Atom. "Thanks to you, I was almost blown to smithereens. Remember your wacky attempt to create the world's safest explosive?" Atom preened his tail. "*I* certainly remember it. Look at these singed feathers!"

"What are *you* complaining about?" the professor asked. "*I* was the one who died in the name of science. It took me more than a hundred years to bring myself sixty-five percent back to life. Then I had to disguise myself as Professor John von Offel and get this position with the Third Millennium Foundation. All that remains is for me to find a way to bring myself fully back to the land of the living."

"I suppose that's where I come in?" Atom asked.

"As always, you'll be an extra set of eyes and ears." The professor grinned and nudged Atom. "Without you, I could never have gotten the chemical formula for Jedidiah Flask's rubber band, eh?"

"Please don't remind me." Atom sighed. "Oh, all right. Let's hear your plan."

The professor chuckled. "As with the best von Offel schemes, this one begins with an unwitting Flask."

"That pigeon-loving teacher?" Atom scoffed.

"Precisely," the professor answered. "Don't be fooled by the fact that Ethan Flask is not a full-time scientist. I was worried at first—after all, as the last remaining Flask, he's my only hope. However, his application for the Vanguard Teacher Award showed definite signs of science genius. Only one day in Ethan Flask's class, and already he's well on his way to helping me. I simply must find a way to make myself fully alive again. It's such a nuisance to be only partly corporeal."

"Cor-what-eal?" Atom asked.

"Corporeal . . . having a solid body!" The professor's expression turned wistful. "I yearn for the little things, like leaving footprints, seeing myself in a mirror, showing up in photographs. These days, I can hardly even remember what I look like!"

"You're not missing much," Atom said dryly. "But that does explain why your hair never looks combed."

"Did you see the chalk drop through my fingers when that rude little ruffian startled me with his snorting?" the professor asked. "What if the children start to suspect?"

"I'm sure nobody noticed." Atom laughed. "Luckily, you bored them all to sleep."

The professor made a face. "I'd like to see you lecture a class full of sixth graders."

"So would I," said Atom. "Maybe Dr. Kepler would hire me to teach biology. No one's ever had a lesson about the animal kingdom straight from the horse's, or rather, parrot's mouth."

"Don't you dare," the professor said. "I have problems enough. Every time I come to a door, I have to concentrate hard just to get a good grip on the doorknob. Otherwise, I'm likely to just sail right through the door!"

"That could be handy if you wanted to get into a locked room," Atom commented. "Just get used to your ghostly existence, and you won't even need me!"

"Impossible! Noncorporeal existence is torture." The professor rubbed his temples. "I can't even get a decent night's rest. Even lying on a bed takes concentration. When I start to fall asleep, I slip right through the mattress. That wakes me up, and I become solid again—just in time to hit the floor!"

Atom stifled a laugh.

"I'm certain I'm on the right track," the professor insisted. "We'll observe young Flask during his study of explosions. He'll soon give away some important clue. Before you know it, I'll be blasting myself fully back into the land of the living."

"Blasting?" Atom squawked. "With your record? Good thing you're already dead."

"I'm not dead," the professor objected. "That is, I'm only thirty-five percent dead. And as long as I concentrate on appearing solid—and don't step in front of any mirrors—no one need ever know."

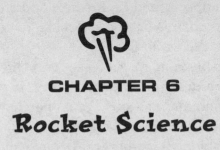

CHAPTER 6

Rocket Science

"I'm here to lodge a formal complaint!" The school custodian stood in front of Mr. Flask, hands on his hips.

"Yes, Mr. Klumpp?" Mr. Flask asked. "Is it about the pigeons yesterday? They didn't drop any . . ." He looked on the floor around him.

"I'm here about explosions!" Mr. Klumpp thundered. "I was silent when your students grew mold gardens. I sat by idly when they were up to their elbows in gooey slime. I twiddled my thumbs as they flung marshmallows with minicatapults. But as the guardian of order and neatness at Einstein Elementary, I must draw a line here and now. No explosions!"

"Science can be messy," Mr. Flask said. "And I realize that you've been very, er, *generous* with your patience. But I promise that all of our explosion experiments will be well controlled."

Mr. Klumpp was unmoved.

"And we have Dr. Kepler's permission," Mr. Flask added.

Mr. Klumpp turned on his heel and stormed out of the classroom—nearly knocking over the sixth graders on their way in.

As the bell sounded, Professor von Offel strode in and sat at a desk in the back corner. He opened his briefcase and placed a small brass perch on the desk for Atom. Then he pulled out a pad of paper, an old-fashioned feather quill pen, and a fancy inkwell. Mr. Flask waited politely.

"Proceed," the professor said impatiently. He dipped his quill into the inkwell.

"Smart scientists always play it safe," Mr. Flask began. "So I'm going to ask Alberta to pass out the safety goggles before I begin my demonstration." Alberta hopped up and headed for the supply cupboard.

"But Mr. Fla-ask, safety goggles leave red lines on my face," Max complained. Sean snickered.

"Try to think of those red marks as the badge of a good scientist, Max," Mr. Flask said. "If you can't, just remember that they fade."

Loud footsteps echoed out in the hall. Mr. Klumpp poked his head through the doorway. He eyed the class suspiciously and stomped away.

"Excuse me, young Flask." The professor cleared his throat. "My inkwell is dry. Could I trouble one of your students for a bottle of ink?"

Alberta sprinted back to her desk, arms full of goggles. "Professor, I don't have a bottle of ink, but I'd be honored to lend you my ballpoint pen." She held it out to him. He frowned. "It's new, so it's completely full of ink," she assured him.

The professor took the pen carefully. He fingered the button at the top, but he didn't click it. He peered into the empty hole at the other end. He shook the pen, then tested it on the paper.

"Young lady, this pen is broken." The professor pushed the pen back at a confused Alberta. "I'm sure I have an extra bottle of ink back in my office." He stalked out of the classroom.

Alberta clicked the pen experimentally. Its point slid into place. From his perch, Atom let out a chuckle-like squawk.

"Luis, Prescott, please help Alberta with the goggles, and let's get under way." Mr. Flask carried a ladder over to a side window. He climbed up and hooked the end of a wire onto a vent in the ceiling. The other end stretched across the classroom to his lab desk.

"Today, we're going to harness the power of an explosion." Mr. Flask returned to his desk and held up a model rocket. "When the chemicals in a model rocket's engine react, the result is definitely exothermic. Sparks fly and hot gases rush out of the nozzle at the bottom. Those gases propel the rocket upward, thanks to Newton's third law of motion. Can anyone remind us what that law is?"

"Don't sit under an apple tree while under the influence of gravity?" Sean asked.

Mr. Flask smiled. "Sean, that's extra credit for

knowing Newton's apple story. Can you share with the class?"

Sean basked in the glory of the class spotlight. "Supposedly, Newton was sitting under an apple tree, just minding his own business. Suddenly, an apple hit him on the head. Newton didn't get mad, though, he got even. He turned that apple into the theory of gravity. He realized that the apple couldn't have moved all by itself. Something had to pull it down—and that something was gravity. Then Newton went home and made apple pie to celebrate."

Mr. Flask laughed. "You're a natural storyteller, Sean. And gravity is definitely part of this rocket's story. Gravity is the force that pulls everything toward the center of our planet. So to blast off into the sky, a rocket has to overcome gravity. It does that using an explosion and, as I said, Newton's third law of motion. That law says: For every force, there is an equal force in the opposite direction. Luis, let's see a few push-ups."

"Huh?" Luis looked startled.

"This isn't a punishment. I just picked you because I know that you can do them, no problem."

Luis shrugged and got down on the floor. "One . . . two . . ."

Mr. Flask gathered the class around. "Luis is using his arms to push down on the floor. But the floor's not going anywhere, right? According to Newton's third law, the floor is actually pushing

Luis back an equal amount. The result? Luis's hands stay put, so his pushing downward raises his body up.

"I brought in some high-tech equipment for this next demonstration." Ethan pulled out two pairs of skates, some helmets, and pads. "Prescott and Alberta, will you please put on this stuff? Now, each of you stand toe to toe. Prescott, your body is the model rocket. Alberta, your body is the gas particles in the exhaust. In a moment, I'm going to ask Alberta to push against Prescott's palms, kind of like a standing push-up. Alberta's pushing arms will represent the force from the exploding chemicals. Okay, push!"

"Whoa!" Alberta and Prescott rolled in opposite directions.

"The energy came from Alberta's arms, our 'exploding chemicals'," Ethan explained. "But because of Newton's third law, Prescott, our 'rocket' and Alberta our 'exhaust' both did the pushing. Each gave and received equal and opposite pushes, which sent them in opposite directions. Now, let's have a round of applause for our three helpers." Alberta and Prescott took off their skates, Luis joined them and all three took a bow.

Ethan put away the skating equipment and hooked the rocket onto the wire. "So, in this experiment, the rocket will be pushed along the wire until it slams into the vent. What do you predict will happen when the chemicals finish reacting?"

Max raised his hand. "We'll take off our goggles?"

"You're single-minded, Max, I'll give you that." Mr. Flask looked around the room. "Another prediction . . . Alberta?"

"The explosion will stop pushing the rocket up. So gravity will pull it back down the wire."

"Okay, let's test that. Everybody move to the back of the classroom, please." Mr. Flask held up a match. "The chemicals in the model rocket engine react when heated. What would happen if I lit the match and held it to the engine?"

Prescott raised his hand. "Kaboom?"

"That's my prediction, too. But let's not test it." Mr. Flask held up a piece of string that was attached to the bottom of the rocket. "Instead, I'll light the end of this fuse. Just like in the movies, the flame will travel up the fuse until it reaches the rocket." He stretched the fuse out to its full length, then lit it. He stepped away. "I like a nice, long fuse for drama, and for safety. Any questions in the next, oh, thirty seconds?"

Just then, Mr. Klumpp burst into the classroom.

"Great! You're just in time to see our first experiment," Mr. Flask said cheerfully.

Mr. Klumpp waved him off. "I'm only here to, uh—" He looked around the room. Then he caught sight of the ladder leading up to the vent. "—check your ceiling vents." He strode across the room and began climbing the ladder. "There's been a phantom knocking sound reported."

Mr. Flask's face went white. "That's not the best place to—"

"Nonsense," Mr. Klumpp cut him short. "I have a great view of your lab—I mean, the vent from up here. I just have to move this wire for a moment."

"But that's our rocket line!" Mr. Flask exclaimed.

Wheeeeest went the rocket as the fuel began to combust.

Mr. Klumpp looked dumbly at the wire in his hand.

"Drop it!" Mr. Flask shouted.

Mr. Klumpp shook the wire out of his hand.

The rocket whizzed up the wire.

"Hit the deck!" Mr. Klumpp shouted, and dove off the ladder.

The rocket reached the end of the falling wire just as the wire passed the open window. The rocket flew out of the classroom and toward a large oak tree.

Mr. Klumpp landed with a tremendous thud. The classroom shook, and the back row of desks left the floor for a moment.

Outside, there was a rustle of leaves and some very surprised chirping.

Mr. Flask sprinted to the back of the classroom. "Are you all right, Mr. Klumpp? Should we call Nurse Daystrom?"

Mr. Klumpp rose with as much dignity as he could muster. "I'm perfectly fine," he said, and stumbled out of the classroom. Just outside the door, he looked around, confused. "Does anybody else hear bells ringing?" Mr. Klumpp whirled around in a circle, then limped away.

A moment later, the professor returned to the classroom, holding a bottle of ink. "Now you may proceed, Flask. I trust I didn't miss anything too earth-shattering."

Mr. Flask opened his mouth, then shut it again.

Alberta spoke up. "Um, nothing worth mentioning, Professor."

Mr. Flask adjusted his goggles. "Perhaps Alberta is right." He took a deep breath, then smiled. "Okay, guys, are you ready to do some more science?"

"Mr. Fla-ask, I don't think I can take another explosion today," Max wailed.

"Fine," Mr. Flask said. He held up a pint of milk and some food coloring. "Prescott, grab some dish detergent from the sink. You and your group are going to do some silent but colorful explosions. Max, I've got an idea for you, too."

"Alberta, you've got a good throwing arm, right? Your group is going to build and explode Popsicle-stick flyers."

The professor turned to Atom. "This is your chance to earn your keep," he whispered. "Get out there and spy on these lab groups."

"Why can't you do some of the dirty work?" Atom hissed.

"I have to keep an eye on Flask," the professor

replied. "After all, *I* am an observer sent by the prestigious Third Millennium Foundation."

Atom surveyed the classroom. "All right, I'll start with the group that has the milk. It's a meal fit only for a cat, but *you* don't feed me enough."

Prescott was dripping food coloring into a bowl of milk. Atom landed on the table next to him. Prescott scrambled away. "Sorry," he said to his lab partners. "My aunt has a bird that bites."

Atom strode over to the bowl and drained as much milk as he could with his beak. Then he lifted the bowl by the rim, getting a surprising amount into his mouth.

"I don't believe it!" Prescott said. "My aunt's bird only eats seeds and stuff. That's one weird parrot."

Atom turned his beady eyes on Prescott. "Awk! Awk! Stupid boy! Stupid boy! Awk! Awk!"

"Funny, my aunt taught her parrot to say that, too," Prescott joked. "Okay, someone shoo that bird away, and I'll set up the experiment again."

In another corner, Max was arguing with Sean. "I simply can't touch that wool," Max insisted. "I may be allergic. My nose will get all itchy and start running." Sean looked annoyed.

"Chill, Sean, let's get going," Heather said smoothly. "Here, catch." She tossed him a pie plate and a cup. Atom swooped in between the two of them and deftly grabbed the cup with his talons. He dropped it into a nearby fish tank, splashing Sean in the process. The boy glared and the parrot strutted away unfazed.

From across the room, Mr. Flask smiled. "Fish out that cup, will you please, Max? Sean, there are more cups in the cabinet. Try again, guys."

Max made a face and cautiously slipped his hand into the fish tank. Sean looked straight at Atom. "Did I ever mention how much I like fried drumsticks?"

Atom stared coolly at each of the lab partners. Then he flicked his tail and flew away.

"Now he's mad at all of us," Max whined.

Outside the classroom, Alberta's group was sitting in a circle on the lawn. Each student was struggling to construct a little flyer out of Popsicle sticks.

"I got it!" Alberta said triumphantly. She held up her flyer for the others to see. "Y'know, each of these sticks is helping to hold the group together. They're all equal in importance. If one was missing, the whole group would fall apart! Doesn't that remind you of our lab group?" She looked up. Two of her lab partners were giving her an exasperated look. The other three were laughing.

Alberta laughed, too. "Okay, I got carried away."

Just then, Atom flew out the window and landed in the middle of their circle.

"I wonder whether the professor knows his bird is out here," Alberta said. "Well, I guess its wings are probably clipped, so it can't go too far. Even with what Mr. Flask said about birdbrains, I still can't imagine this thing is very bright."

Atom strutted up to Alberta and ripped her Popsicle-stick flyer out of her hands. He flipped it up and balanced it on his beak for a few moments. Then he slipped it around his body and used it like a hula hoop. Finally, he let it fall to the ground, picked it up with one claw, and sent it sailing toward the trunk of a tree. The flyer hit the tree and "exploded" with a satisfying *crack*.

Atom flew to the windowsill and paused to look at the group. Alberta shrugged and looked at her lab partners. "I guess I take it back."

The professor sat at his desk, taking notes. Atom landed beside him.

"What did you learn?" the professor whispered.

"That sixth graders haven't changed in a hundred-thirteen years," Atom sniffed. "They still think they're smarter than their elders."

The professor leaned toward Atom. "You didn't show them otherwise, did you?"

Atom pointed to himself with one wing. "Who, me? No way. Anyway, I've got something to do." He flew back over to Prescott's table. He noted with pleasure how Prescott scrambled away once again. Then he strode over to the bowl of milk and emptied it—food coloring, dishwashing detergent, and all. He gave a satisfied burp, and a bubble popped out of his beak. He chuckled as it floated away.

CHAPTER 7

Eye Spy

"Luis, Alberta, Prescott!" Mr. Flask caught the lab assistants in the hallway after class. "I have an extracurricular favor to ask you. Dr. Kepler wants some student entertainment at the PTA meeting on Thursday night. Since the sixth graders have been studying chemical reactions, I thought you might demonstrate one."

"This doesn't involve exploding any rocket fuel, does it?" Prescott asked.

Mr. Flask laughed. "No, just exploding a zip-up plastic bag full of gases. No combustion, I promise."

"Okay, I'm up for it," Prescott said. The other two nodded.

"Great! Meet me after school on Thursday."

The lab assistants headed outside.

"I feel sorry for Mr. Flask already," Prescott said. "If the rest of the Third Millennium Foundation is as weird as the professor, Mr. Flask can kiss the Vanguard Teacher Award good-bye."

"The professor does seem a little strange," Alberta admitted. "I mean, nobody writes with a quill anymore. And did you see when I handed him my ballpoint pen? He looked at it like it was the robotic arm of the space shuttle."

"How about that monocle he wears?" Luis added. "Where do you even buy one of those anymore?"

"And what's up with that parrot?" Prescott asked. "Did you notice how all the other animals seem to hate him? And when Mr. Klumpp nearly got beaned with that rocket, I swear I heard that bird say 'Yikes!'"

"You should have seen the acrobatic tricks he put on for my lab group," Alberta said. "It almost seemed like he was showing off."

"I'm not surprised. He was drinking my lab group's experiment!" Prescott said. "And he seems to know that I'm scared of birds."

"They say that a lot of animals can sense fear—like dogs," Alberta added.

"Yeah, but I think this bird actually enjoys it!" said Prescott. "And I still say that chalk fell *through* the professor's fingers."

"What are you talking about?" Luis asked.

"Oh, Prescott thinks the professor is a ghost," Alberta said.

"I didn't say that," said Prescott. "At least, not out loud."

"Well, whatever the professor is, he's still a von Offel. Maybe he'll be impressed enough with our PTA performance that we can get him to write each of us a college recommendation."

"Six years early?" Luis asked.

Alberta shrugged. "It always pays to think ahead."

"Only up to a point!" said Luis.

"Wait!" Prescott stopped. "Isn't that the professor ahead of us? Looks like that parrot on his shoulder. I wonder where he's going."

"He's probably just walking home," Alberta said.

"I say we follow the professor and see if we can learn more about him," said Prescott.

"You want to spy on him?" Luis asked.

"Don't you?" Prescott replied.

"Let's not think of it as spying," Alberta said. "Let's call it investigating."

"Whatever," Prescott said. "Just stay back and act casual."

A group of school buses rolled by. Sean leaned out of a bus window far ahead. He wound up his arm to pitch a candy bar wrapper at Atom. The bird was too fast, though. Atom fluttered up into the air just as the silvery ball left Sean's hand. The professor looked up, clearly startled, at the fast-moving wad. But a second later, the wrapper landed harmlessly on the grass.

"Did you see that?" Prescott asked.

Luis shook his head. "Yeah, Sean has some nerve littering."

"I mean, that candy wrapper passed right through the professor's body!" Prescott cried.

Alberta made a face. "How could you tell?"

"Sean is usually a good shot," Prescott reasoned. "He's on the baseball team. If he aimed at the professor and his parrot, he should have hit them! But he missed. The only explanation is that the wrapper passed through the professor's body."

"I don't know, Prescott," Luis said. "I think that's a stretch. Even major league pitchers don't always hit the strike zone."

"Well, I'm just telling you what I saw," Prescott replied. "It looked like the candy wrapper passed through the professor's chest and landed behind him."

"I believe that's what you saw," Alberta said quietly. "But remember what Mr. Flask said about the brain making you hear what you want to hear? Maybe it can also make you see what you want to see."

The professor had stopped to shake his fist at the bus. The lab assistants held back for a moment. When the professor started walking again, they followed slowly, matching his pace.

The professor's pace was very slow. Luis started to get impatient.

"This is taking forever! What are we watching for, anyway?" he asked.

"Maybe he'll stop at a phone booth," Prescott said. "If he does, we have to get close enough to see the phone number he dials."

"How would that number help us?" Alberta asked.

"I don't know," Prescott admitted. "I guess I'd be too scared to dial it anyway."

"Hey, he's stopping!" Alberta said. She put out her arms to hold Prescott and Luis back.

Professor von Offel was looking in the window of a grocery store. Atom was pecking on the glass with his beak. The professor shook his head. Atom started hopping up and down and flapping his wings furiously. Finally, the professor threw up his hands and walked to the store's entrance. He pushed against one of the doors, but it didn't budge.

"Could the grocery store possibly be closed in the middle of the afternoon?" Prescott asked.

"My mom shops there," said Luis, pointing toward the store. "She drags me there at all hours. It's always open."

"Wait," said Alberta. "Doesn't the store have those automatic doors? Just standing on that mat in front of the entrance should make them slide open."

The professor raised his fist to knock. Behind him, a woman rolled a stroller onto the mat. The doors whooshed open, and the professor jumped back. He peered into the store cautiously. The woman with the stroller barreled by him. The professor took a timid step into the store, and the doors clunked shut behind him.

"You didn't believe me about the chalk or the candy wrapper," Prescott said. "But both of you saw *that* incriminating evidence. His ghostly body can't even activate an automatic door!"

Luis and Alberta were both silent.

"Well?" Prescott demanded.

"I'm sorry, but I just have to be more skeptical than that," Alberta said. "Maybe his feet just missed the sensors."

Prescott threw up his hands. He stormed over to the mat, bent down, and pushed it with one finger. The doors flew open. He waited until they shut. Then he poked the mat in a different spot. The doors flew open again. He let them shut. Then he poked the mat in another spot. The doors flew open a third time. This time they didn't shut. Prescott looked up. Towering over him was a very irritated cashier.

"Every day, it's the same thing!" she scolded. "Open, shut, open, shut. You kids are driving me crazy! Now get out of here, or I'll march you right back to school and straight into the principal's office."

Prescott's face turned pale. "But I was just—I never . . ."

The cashier turned to Alberta and Luis. "I suppose he was putting on this little show for you. Well, I want all three of you out of here. And I warn you—I never forget a face!"

The lab assistants hurried up the sidewalk to the next corner. When they turned around, the cashier was gone.

"I'm done for," Luis said. "Like I said, my mom drags me in there all the time. That cashier is always there, and she's really friendly with my mom. What's she going to say next time we're in there?"

"If she really never forgets a face," Alberta said, "why didn't she recognize you this time?"

"Hey, here comes the professor!" Prescott pushed the other two around the corner.

"I'm done spying for today," Luis said.

"Okay," said Prescott. "But we can at least stand here as he walks by and try to notice what's in his bag. Now, act casual." He looked at his nails and began to whistle.

"Oh, *that's* convincing," Luis said.

The professor was angry when he reached the corner. "Oh, for heaven's sakes!" he shouted at Atom. "Have it your way!" He reached into his shopping bag and pulled out a box of bird seed. He jammed the empty bag into his pocket. Then he ripped off the box top and poured a pile of bird seed onto the sidewalk.

Atom hopped to the ground and began devouring the seed. The professor tucked the box under his arm and walked away. Atom finished the pile, then flew after him.

Luis tapped his temple. "Let's put on our thinking caps. The professor bought *bird seed*. That evidence suggests he has a *bird*." He threw up his hands. "Which is the one thing we already know about him!"

"Okay, so we didn't find out anything useful," Alberta said. "At least we tried."

Prescott was still watching the professor walk away. "I'm less interested in what he bought than in what he didn't buy."

"What do you mean?" Alberta asked.

"Well, if he'd bought a snack, I'd have to admit that he's not a ghost. After all, ghosts don't eat, right?" Prescott explained. "But all he bought was bird seed. I think that could be very telling."

Luis rolled his eyes. Alberta just hid a little smile.

CHAPTER 8

Fungus Among Us

M r. Flask stood behind his lab desk. He arranged a slice of bread, a packet of yeast, a bag of sugar, a beaker of water, an empty pop bottle, and a cork in front of him.

"What is this, the Cooking Channel?" Sean called out. He plopped into his seat and slipped a hard candy into his mouth just as the bell rang. "At least we're finally going to experiment with sugar."

The professor's eyes narrowed in disapproval. His quill twitched.

Mr. Flask just smiled. "I'm glad I got your attention, Sean." He held up the packet of yeast. "These little creatures have a sweet tooth that you could appreciate."

"Creatures?" asked Alberta. "There are living things in there?"

"*Saccharomyces cerevisiae*," Mr. Flask answered. "It's a kind of fungus."

"But, Mr. Fla-ask!" Max whined. "My mother told me never to touch fungus."

"That may be," Mr. Flask replied. "But I bet you had this fungus for lunch."

Heather Patterson wrinkled her perfect nose. "Ewwwwwh!"

"But I made my own turkey sandwich—and I washed my hands first!" Max looked upset.

Mr. Flask held up the slice of bread from his lab table. "Did you use bread?"

"Of course," Max answered.

"Do you see these little, tiny pockets of air in this bread?"

Max nodded.

"Yeast put them there."

Luis raised his hand. "My uncle is a baker. He told me about this. When yeast eats, it makes a gas called carbon dioxide. Bakers mix yeast and sugar into bread dough. When the yeast releases gas, the dough rises—it gets bigger. Then when you bake it into bread, it's soft and spongy."

"I've always said that baking is a science," said Mr. Flask. He ripped open the yeast packet and poured the contents into the empty pop bottle. "Today, we're going to treat these little guys to a sugar feast. They're going to party hard and show us some explosive, air-expanding action."

The classroom door swung open with a bang. A figure burst in, outfitted for a bomb squad. It was covered from head to toe with heavy rain gear. It wore welding goggles, a gas mask, and the kind of earmuffs worn by airline mechanics. It carried a thick, clear shield on one arm.

"Mr. Klumpp?" Mr. Flask asked. "Is that you?"

Mr. Klumpp's voice was muffled. "I'm back to work on the vent." He shuffled back to the ladder, but he didn't climb it. Instead, he stood peering at Mr. Flask through the shield.

"Um, okay, party time." Mr. Flask held up the bottle so the class could see the yeast. "First, some warm water to wake up the *Saccharomyces cerevisiae*. Now, for the snacks." He spooned in some sugar. He popped the cork back in the bottle and swirled the mixture around in the bottle. "Having a good time in there, guys?"

Suddenly, Mr. Klumpp stormed forward, his shield held out in front of him. "Duck under your desks and cover your heads!" he shouted. He shot out with a pair of salad tongs and ripped the bottle from Mr. Flask's hand. "Stay calm—I'll take the full blow myself!" He aimed the bottle at his shield and gritted his teeth.

Ping! The cork flew lazily out of the bottle. It gave Mr. Klumpp's armored shield a gentle tap.

The class dissolved into laughter. Even Mr. Flask had trouble keeping a straight face.

Mr. Klumpp lowered the bottle onto the lab table. Without a word, he slunk out of the classroom.

As he went, his shield knocked Heather Patterson's desk, spilling her books onto the floor. She folded her arms, waiting, and about a dozen boys rushed to pick up her things. As they scrambled around, her books and papers scattered farther. Heather just sat back and enjoyed the attention.

A sports magazine landed at the professor's feet. An old Chicago Bulls photo of Michael Jordan smiled from the cover, under the words "Athlete of the Millennium."

The professor picked it up and studied the photo. Finally, he held it out to Heather and demanded, "Who is this bald gentleman and why does he have the number 23 on his undershirt?"

Later that day, Luis caught up with Prescott and Alberta on their way to English class. "How can anyone not know who Michael Jordan is?" he asked. "You'd have to be living in a cave for twenty years."

"Or since people wrote with quills!" Alberta added. "We've got to find out more about this guy—just for Mr. Flask's sake."

"Okay, let's approach this scientifically," Luis said.

"What are we going to do, X-ray his skull?" Prescott asked.

"I mean, let's make a hypothesis. Then let's think of a way to test it," Luis said.

"My hypothesis is that the professor is a ghost who's been out of touch with the world for a way long time," Prescott said. "My evidence is that, number one, he writes with a feather. And number two, he didn't recognize Michael Jordan, possibly the most famous person in the world. Isn't that enough? I'm not even counting the chalk and the automatic door incidents."

"I don't know if that's enough," Luis said. "That evidence could mean something else. Like, what if he's too wrapped up in scientific research to follow sports? And what if he just likes the feel of a quill pen?"

"We've got to find a way to collect more evidence," Alberta agreed. "But we can't just walk up and quiz him about current events. Can we?"

Prescott smiled. "I just thought of a plan. But it doesn't involve science. It's pure social studies—plus a little drama."

After English class, the lab assistants tracked down the professor. They put Prescott's plan in motion.

"Excuse me, Professor! Could you help us with an assignment?" Alberta smiled brightly and held up her clipboard.

The professor stood at the door to his office and eyed them suspiciously. Atom perched on his shoulder, looking bored.

"About explosions, is it?" he asked. "Is Mr. Flask unable to answer your questions?"

"Actually, we're doing a unit on public opinion in social studies," Prescott answered. "We're supposed to interview someone."

"I'm very busy, young man," the professor said.

"That's great!" Alberta said, "because it has to be someone busy and important . . . someone whose opinion counts."

"Awwwwwwk!" Atom coughed and almost lost his footing. The professor snatched Atom off his shoulder and plopped him on a perch inside the office. Then he stepped out into the hallway and closed the door.

"In that case," the professor said, "proceed."

"What is your opinion of the Internet?" Luis began.

"The Internet is an idea whose time has come," the professor answered.

Alberta raised her eyebrows at Prescott. Maybe the professor wasn't completely out to lunch after all.

"It's about time that fishermen pooled their resources," the professor continued. "After all, the larger the net, the more fish they can catch."

Prescott smiled back at Alberta. Then he turned to the professor. "In your opinion, how important is the Super Bowl?"

"It's very important to those studying Egyptian pottery. For the rest of us, I'm not sure how important any one large pot is," the professor answered.

"What is the future of HBO?" Alberta asked.

The professor bared his teeth in a smile. "Has Mr. Flask been singing the praises of Hydroboricoxide? It must be, I mean, it *is* a very valuable chemical. Scientists will no doubt find many uses for it. I may experiment with HBO myself."

"What is the top speed humans will achieve?" Luis asked.

"Mark my words, it's just a matter of time before scientists can propel a man faster than forty miles per hour." The professor frowned. "Some would propose safety tests using chickens first, but I say we should move boldly."

"How has Velcro affected our lives?" Prescott asked.

The professor shook his head impatiently. "It is a pity for farmers that the Vell crow has run amok in our nation's cornfields. However, with construction of new Vell scarecrows, the average person need not find his life much changed."

"What should NASA do next?" Alberta asked.

"That's 'nah-saw,' young lady. Doesn't your geography teacher test your pronunciation? I have no opinion whatsoever about what Nassau—or any city in the Bahamas—should do next. Perhaps provide its residents with parasols during the sunny summer days?" Now the professor looked truly irritated. "Does that satisfy your needs?"

Alberta managed a smile. "Yes, thank you Professor."

"We certainly got what we were looking for," added Luis.

"Then good day, children," the professor said stiffly. He turned on his heel and retreated into his office.

The lab assistants were silent until they got halfway down the hall.

"Think we've got enough evidence?" Prescott asked.

"I'd say we've established that his top speed hasn't approached forty miles per hour since the days of the steam engine," Luis said.

"When people wrote with quills," Alberta added.

CHAPTER 9

Mission Im-barrassing

Prescott poked his head out of the boys' bathroom. The hallway was empty. School was over, and Prescott had just heard the last bus pull away. Still, you could never be too careful. He looked both ways, then slipped out into the hallway, a big lump under his shirt. Prescott could feel his heart beating. Around the corner came a kindergartner and his mother. Would they notice the weird lump? No, they didn't give Prescott a second look—the mom was too busy oohing and ahhing over a seed collage.

In the middle of the next hallway, Prescott's English teacher and math teacher stood talking. Prescott clutched the lump closer. There was no turning back now—Prescott had to pass them. As he came closer, his teachers turned and smiled. Prescott bent over and coughed so they wouldn't see the lump.

"Are you okay, Prescott?" his English teacher asked. Prescott held up a hand to show that he was. When he got well past the two teachers, he straightened up. Only one more hallway until Mr. Flask's classroom. Prescott turned the corner. There was no one in sight. He picked up his pace. Almost home safe! But as he passed the social studies classroom, a voice called out.

"Hi, Prescott. What've you got there?"

It was Heather Patterson!

Prescott's face turned red and his mouth hung open. He raced down the hall and into Mr. Flask's classroom. Prescott plopped something down onto the teacher's desk. Mr. Flask looked up from the stack of papers he was reading.

"Mr. Flask, please don't ever ask me to bring you toilet paper again!" said Prescott. Then he blushed deeply.

"Thanks, Prescott. Sorry if it was any trouble." Mr. Flask pulled off three squares of toilet paper and placed them on the table.

"You only needed three squares?" Prescott cried. "I went all *Mission Impossible* for three squares?"

"Well, these are just for practice," Mr. Flask said. "We'll need another three squares for tonight."

Just then, Alberta and Luis struggled through the doorway with a large tub.

"I didn't think Mr. Klumpp was going to let us borrow this," Alberta said. "But then Luis told him that it would prevent a big mess during the PTA meeting."

Mr. Flask spooned baking soda onto each square of toilet paper. Then he gathered the corners of each square and twisted. "I'm thinking of calling this experiment 'Booming Bags.' You'll have to tell me what you think." He handed each lab assistant a zip-up plastic bag.

"Should we hold these over the tub?" Luis asked.

Mr. Flask nodded. He poured vinegar into each bag. Then he handed each lab assistant a twisted-up, baking-soda-filled toilet-paper wad. "Slip the wad of baking soda into the bag, but don't let it touch the vinegar. The tricky part is holding it near the top while you zip up the plastic bag."

After a few moments of concentration, the bags were all zipped.

"In a minute, I'll ask you to let the baking soda fall into the vinegar," Mr. Flask said. "The two chemicals will react and produce carbon dioxide gas."

"Isn't that the same gas that the yeast gave off?" Alberta asked.

"Exactly! This time the process is chemical instead of biological. But the result is the same. Ready? Set? Go!"

Mr. Klumpp picked this moment to poke his head into the room.

"Flask, I've scrubbed that cafeteria spotless for the PTA meeting," he said. The lab assistants saw their plastic bags inflate with gas. Mr. Klumpp ranted on as the bags stretched tighter and tighter. "If this experiment of yours makes too much of a mess . . ."

Pop! Pop! Pop! The plastic bags burst in rapid succession. With each pop, Mr. Klumpp jumped as if he'd been stuck with a pin. He turned to face the lab assistants. Foamy liquid spewed out of ripped seams—and luckily, splashed into the tub. The smell of vinegar filled the air. Veins stood out on Mr. Klumpp's bald head.

"Dr. Kepler will hear about this!" he declared, and stomped out.

Dr. Kepler sat at her desk, reviewing her PTA remarks. Mr. Klumpp knocked at the open door, and she waved him in.

"The chairs are set up in the cafeteria, but the coffee and refreshments haven't arrived," Mr. Klumpp said. "And I think we have a bigger problem. Ethan Flask and his students are planning an outrageous . . ."

"No coffee or refreshments?" Dr. Kepler cut him off. "That's the *biggest* problem possible when you have a cafeteria full of hungry parents. This could get ugly."

She picked up the phone and dialed. After a short conversation, she turned back to Mr. Klumpp. "Food Services insists they've made the delivery. That food is in the building somewhere. Find it."

"But, the issue with Flask . . ." Mr. Klumpp protested.

"Yes, yes, I know his Booming Plastic Bags experiment is a little messy. But it's good science." She waved Mr. Klumpp toward the door. "Now, please go find that food. The parents will be here any minute!"

Over in the cafeteria, Alberta spooned baking soda onto three squares of toilet paper. "This will be the smash hit of the PTA meeting!" she said. Prescott and Luis struggled to empty the big plastic tub into the lab sink. "If we spill any of this stuff on Mr. Klumpp's cafeteria floor, he may smash hit us," said Prescott.

Mr. Flask picked up the vinegar and plastic bags. "Okay, let's go dazzle 'em with science!" He held the door as Luis and Prescott struggled with the big plastic tub. Alberta finished twisting up the baking soda bundles and ran to catch up, shutting the door to the classroom behind her.

Minutes later, the door opened a crack. An eye, framed by a monocle, peered in.

"Excellent, Flask's laboratory is free," said the professor. He pushed open the door and wheeled in a large machine on a cart. Atom fluttered in and landed on the machine. The professor locked the door behind them.

Atom stepped carefully across a mass of wires and peered into a dusty vacuum tube. Above him, a radar dish teetered unsteadily.

"This looks about as professional as a pigeon's nest. Are you going to tell me what's going on?" asked the parrot.

"I've pinpointed the type of explosion we'll need

to bring my body the rest of the way back into this world," the professor answered. "I told you Ethan Flask would lead me to it!"

Atom tapped the radar dish with his beak. "I don't recall seeing this in Flask's class."

"Of course, his dull little Flask mind wouldn't think on a scale this grand," the professor replied. "But Flask hit on something when he demonstrated the explosive life force of yeast."

"Wasn't that just a bunch of fungi eating and burping?" asked Atom.

"To an untrained mind, yes," the professor answered. "But I tweaked the idea and built upon it, and this is the result."

"And just what is it?" Atom asked.

The professor smiled proudly. "An ultrasonic generator, which will stimulate the seeds within a watermelon to vibrate at a great velocity."

Atom shook his head. "Yes, this *sounds* like the work of the brain that turned Jedidiah Flask's simple rubber band into the crazy rubber eight."

The professor ignored him. "According to my calculations, when the vibrations reach the speed of light, they will annihilate the watermelon. I'll be bombarded with seeds, which will hit me with such force that they will transmit their life energy into my body."

"Oh, that'll work!" Atom scoffed. "And what am I supposed to do when you turn yourself into the world's largest watermelon smoothie?"

"You could always go work for your precious Flasks," the professor said. "Maybe after a few weeks with that boring Ethan character you'll be ready to appreciate my true genius." He snatched up a two-foot-long pole with a small capsule on one end. "If you'll excuse me, I have science to do." He unlocked the door and stormed out. Atom sighed and flew after him.

The professor walked a few yards down the hall and disappeared into a storeroom. Atom slipped in just before the storeroom door slammed shut. He perched on a stack of paper towels.

The professor turned to Atom with a satisfied smile. "Under this sheet is the largest watermelon ever to be grown in this state. It is four feet long, three feet wide, and weighs two hundred and seventy pounds. It contains an estimated fifteen-hundred seeds." He drew back the cloth and stabbed the pole he was carrying into the watermelon's side. Then the professor withdrew the pole and showed Atom that the capsule remained inside. "A transceiver—a radio connection between this watermelon and my ultrasonic generator," he explained.

CHAPTER 10

A Fifteen-Hundred-Seed Salute?

The school cafeteria was abuzz. "Five minutes late! Don't they know how much baby-sitters charge?"

"At preschool parent meetings, we always had a gourmet dinner! And it was always on time!"

"I'd like to see that principal sit on one of these tiny chairs without *her* bottom falling asleep!"

PTA president Mrs. Ratner bravely faced the grumbling mob. "I'm sure Dr. Kepler will be here soon. In the meantime, I'll find Mr. Klumpp. At least he'll know where the refreshments are." She rushed out the side door.

Meanwhile, Atom stood on Mr. Flask's desk, flipping through his lesson plans and teaching notes. "Hey, you should read this! Not a single watermelon experiment in here!"

"Quiet, you pompous piece of poultry," the professor mumbled. He hovered over his ultrasonic generator, setting dials and toggles. Then he straightened up and flipped a switch. The small radar dish wobbled and began to turn slowly.

Atom fluttered over. "What now?"

"The machine is projecting energy to the transceiver. It will take a full ten minutes for the seeds to vibrate at the speed of light. That will allow plenty of time for me to strap myself to the watermelon." The professor looked around. "Now, where is that duct tape?"

Mr. Klumpp stalked down the hall, grumbling to himself. "'The food is in the building somewhere,' she says. 'Find it,' she says. Well, I've searched every inch of this school, and there's no food to be found. I defy her to find so much as a minimuffin within these walls!"

Suddenly, he stopped short. The storeroom door was slightly ajar. Surely, Food Services wouldn't deliver refreshments to a science storage closet? He looked inside. "A watermelon? What a stupid idea for a snack. Well, it certainly looks big enough to feed fifty parents." He fought to roll the ungainly fruit into the hallway.

Back in the cafeteria, Prescott leaned over towards Alberta and Luis.

"The competition is going to be fiercer than I thought," he whispered. He pointed to the area where the students and their teachers were waiting to perform. "Those kindergartners in the taste-bud costumes will get major points for cuteness."

"This is a science demonstration, not a contest,"

Alberta replied. She watched another kindergartner skip by with a giant felt ice-cream cone. "They do look like a hard act to follow, though."

"At least we're not like those poor third graders," Luis put in. "All they have is a poster board covered with cutout magazine photos. *That* teacher gets a C minus for effort."

"Attention, everyone!" Dr. Kepler stood at the door. "Thanks for your patience. Still no sign of the refreshments, but we're going to begin the meeting."

Mr. Flask was standing with a group of teachers. "Dr. Kepler?" he interrupted. "Would you like me to send my lab assistants out for refreshments? The grocery store is only a few blocks away. Just jot down a shopping list. I know these guys are responsible enough to handle the job."

Prescott's eyes grew wide. He looked at Alberta and Luis and made a face.

"Thanks, Mr. Flask." Dr. Kepler smiled at the lab assistants. "But your sixth graders are up first."

"That was a close one," Prescott whispered.

Mr. Flask broke away from a group of teachers and joined the lab assistants. Dr. Kepler followed. "Ethan, will Professor von Offel be in the audience?"

"I'm not sure," Mr. Flask said.

"Maybe there's enough time to send one of your lab assistants to find him," Dr. Kepler said. "After all, I want him to get every chance to see what a fantastic teacher you are."

Mr. Flask frowned as Dr. Kepler walked away.

"I'll take care of this myself," he said. "I suppose I should have invited the professor in the first place. Somehow, he and I have really gotten off on the wrong foot."

"About the professor—" Prescott began.

Luis shook his head. This wasn't the time or place to go into their "opinion poll" results.

While Prescott struggled with his doubts about the professor, Mr. Klumpp struggled with a much more immediate problem. The giant watermelon wobbled from one side of the hallway to the other as Mr. Klumpp pushed it toward the cafeteria. "Next time, they better order something lighter—or at least something rounder." Mr. Klumpp grunted. "This is killing my back!"

The custodian stopped just outside the cafeteria door and squatted down to rest for a moment. He leaned against the watermelon for support. Warmth and vibrations soothed his lower back muscles. *Mmmmmm*, that felt good. Wait a second! Mr. Klumpp turned around and touched the rind— could this giant watermelon really be heating up and vibrating?

Mrs. Ratner stormed up behind him. "That? That's refreshments?" she sputtered. "What are we supposed to do? Push it down the aisle and ask people to take a bite as it wheels by?"

"There's something a little funny about this . . ."

"No kidding!" Mrs. Ratner said nastily. "Let's just get it inside."

Mr. Klumpp heaved the watermelon end over end through the narrow cafeteria door. Then he and Mrs. Ratner steered it between the rows of chairs to the front of the room. The room grew silent, except for a growing chorus of oohs and aahs. Parents left their seats to gawk at the enormous fruit.

"What a watermelon!" Mr. Flask said to himself as he passed by. He headed down the corridor in search of the professor. "I wonder what fertilizer the farmer used? Maybe we could do a school garden in the spring . . ."

The professor and Atom stood in the doorway of the empty storeroom.

The professor was waving a roll of duct tape wildly. His face was beet-red. "Where's my watermelon?" he bellowed.

"You know," said Atom, "you really should see someone about controlling your anger."

The professor whipped around his pocket watch by the chain.

"Only thirty seconds to detonation!"

Mr. Flask rounded the corner. "Ah, there you are, Professor. I was hoping you'd come watch our students perform an experiment for the PTA meeting. They're ready to start. Mr. Klumpp is just hunting up some plates to serve the watermelon."

The professor's face turned purple. "No-o-o-o-o!"

Back in the cafeteria, the lab assistants were ready to go. "When we drop the baking soda into the vinegar, the two chemicals will begin to react," Luis explained to the crowd. Dr. Kepler stood to one side, smiling proudly.

Mr. Klumpp approached the watermelon with a large knife.

"One by-product of the reaction will be carbon dioxide gas," Prescott continued. "That's the same gas we exhale. And it's the gas that makes soda fizzy."

Mr. Klumpp touched the watermelon. The vibrating rind shivered under his fingers.

"As more and more carbon dioxide is produced, the air pressure inside the plastic bag will increase," Alberta added. "The plastic bag will puff up. Finally, the pressure will cause the plastic bag to explode."

Mr. Klumpp squinted at the watermelon. Could he actually *see* it quaking now?

"Better cover your ears!" Luis joked. The parents laughed. "Okay—one, two, three, go!" The lab assistants let the wads of baking soda fall into the vinegar.

There was only one thing for Mr. Klumpp to do. He raised his knife to split open the giant fruit.

In a split second: The plastic bags swelled up with carbon dioxide, Mr. Klumpp thrust his knife into the watermelon, and Professor von Offel burst into the cafeteria with Atom flapping wildly behind.

BOOOOM! The world turned pink. When the air cleared, the walls, the floor, the parents—everything and everybody—dripped with watermelon gunk. A fine gray powder smelling of burned seeds was dusted over it all.

A Food Services employee rushed in, pushing a hand truck stacked with boxes. His jaw dropped.

Dr. Kepler filled the stunned silence. "I think we already ate."

The next day, the lab assistants took their seats in science class.

"Is it my imagination, or is the professor glaring at us?" Prescott asked.

"It's hard to tell when he's wearing that monocle," Luis answered. "But you should have seen the look he gave Mr. Flask when he came in."

"I bet this has to do with last night," Prescott said.

"But the professor can't possibly think that *we're* responsible," Alberta said. "We were hit the hardest! I showered for an hour last night and I still smell like fruit salad!"

"And how weird is this?" Luis added. "Mr. Flask just told me that nobody even ordered that watermelon. So where did it come from?"

"Well, I for one think it was the professor's," said Prescott. "Did you notice how he and that creepy bird came running in right before the watermelon went off? Was that just a coincidence?"

Alberta glanced back at the professor. "Well, we know one thing for sure. Strange stuff happens all around him. He's a real 'awful von Offel,' all right!"

Welcome to the World of
MAD SCIENCE!

The Mad Science Group has been providing live, interactive, exciting science experiences for children throughout the world for more than 12 years. Our goal is to provide children with fun, entertaining and exciting activities that instill a clearer understanding of what science is really about and how it affects the world around them. Founded in Montreal, Canada, we currently have 125 locations throughout the world.

Our commitment to science education is demonstrated throughout this imaginative series that mixes hilarious fiction with factual information to show how science plays an important role in our daily lives. To add to the learning fun, we've also created exciting, accessible experiment logs so that children can bring the excitement of hands-on science right into their homes.

To discover more about Mad Science and how
to bring our interactive science experience to your
home or school, check out our website:
http://www.madscience.org

We spark the imagination and curiosity
of children everywhere!